THE
CONSEQUENCES
OF SYRIA

HERBERT AND JANE DWIGHT WORKING GROUP
ON ISLAMISM AND THE INTERNATIONAL ORDER

*Many of the writings associated with this
Working Group will be published by the Hoover Institution.
Materials published to date, or in production, are listed below.*

[For a list of books published under the auspices of the
WORKING GROUP ON ISLAMISM AND THE INTERNATIONAL ORDER,
please see page 57.]

THE
CONSEQUENCES
OF SYRIA

Lee Smith

HOOVER INSTITUTION PRESS
Stanford University   Stanford, California

The Hoover Institution on War, Revolution and Peace, founded at Stanford University in 1919 by Herbert Hoover, who went on to become the thirty-first president of the United States, is an interdisciplinary research center for advanced study on domestic and international affairs. The views expressed in its publications are entirely those of the authors and do not necessarily reflect the views of the staff, officers, or Board of Overseers of the Hoover Institution.

www.hoover.org

Hoover Institution Press Publication No. 651

Hoover Institution at Leland Stanford Junior University, Stanford, California, 94305-6010

Copyright © 2014 by the Board of Trustees of the
    Leland Stanford Junior University
All rights reserved. No part of this publication may be reproduced, stored in a retrieval system, or transmitted in any form or by any means, electronic, mechanical, photocopying, recording, or otherwise, without written permission of the publisher and copyright holders.

For permission to reuse material from *The Consequences of Syria*, by Lee Smith, ISBN 978-0-8179-1775-3, please access www.copyright.com or contact the Copyright Clearance Center, Inc. (CCC), 222 Rosewood Drive, Danvers, MA 01923, 978-750-8400. CCC is a not-for-profit organization that provides licenses and registration for a variety of uses.

First printing 2014
21 20 19 18 17 16 15 14   9 8 7 6 5 4 3 2 1

Manufactured in the United States of America

The paper used in this publication meets the minimum requirements of the American National Standard for Information Sciences—Permanence of Paper for Printed Library Materials, ANSI/NISO Z39.48-1992. ⊗

Cataloging-in-Publication Data is available from the Library of Congress.
ISBN 978-0-8179-1775-3 (pbk.: alk. paper)
ISBN 978-0-8179-1776-0 (epub)
ISBN 978-0-8179-1777-7 (mobi)
ISBN 978-0-8179-1778-4 (PDF)

*The Hoover Institution gratefully acknowledges
the following individuals and foundations
for their significant support of the*

HERBERT AND JANE DWIGHT WORKING GROUP
ON ISLAMISM AND THE INTERNATIONAL ORDER:

Herbert and Jane Dwight

Beall Family Foundation

Stephen Bechtel Foundation

Lynde and Harry Bradley Foundation

Mr. and Mrs. Clayton W. Frye Jr.

Lakeside Foundation

CONTENTS

The Great Unraveling: The Remaking of the Middle East

IT'S A MANTRA, but it is also true: the Middle East is being unmade and remade. The autocracies that gave so many of these states the appearance of stability are gone, their dreaded rulers dispatched to prison or exile or cut down by young people who had yearned for the end of the despotisms. These autocracies were large prisons, and in 2011, a storm overtook that stagnant world. The spectacle wasn't pretty, but prison riots never are. In the Fertile Crescent, the work of the colonial cartographers—Gertrude Bell, Winston Churchill, and Georges Clemenceau— are in play as they have never been before. Arab nationalists were given to lamenting that they lived in nation-states "invented" by Western powers in the aftermath of the Great War. Now, a century later, with the ground burning in Lebanon, Syria, and Iraq and the religious sects at war, not even the most ardent nationalists can be sure that they can put in place anything better than the old order.

Men get used to the troubles they know, and the Greater Middle East seems fated for grief and breakdown. Outside powers approach it with dread; merciless political contenders have the run of it. There is swagger in Iran and a belief that the radical theocracy can bully its rivals into submission. There was a period when the United States provided a modicum of order in these Middle Eastern lands. But pleading fatigue, and financial scarcity at home, we have all but announced the end of that stewardship. We are poorer for that abdication, and the Middle East is thus left to the mercy of predators of every kind.

We asked a number of authors to give this spectacle of disorder their best try. We imposed no rules on them, as we were sure their essays would take us close to the sources of the malady.

FOUAD AJAMI
Senior Fellow, Hoover Institution—
Cochairman, Herbert and Jane Dwight Working Group
on Islamism and the International Order

CHARLES HILL
Distinguished Fellow of the Brady-Johnson Program
in Grand Strategy at Yale University;
Research Fellow, Hoover Institution—
Cochairman, Herbert and Jane Dwight Working Group
on Islamism and the International Order

The Consequences of Syria

LEE SMITH

I: LOOKING AT SYRIA, SEEING IRAQ

SINCE AUGUST 2011 when he demanded that Bashar al-Assad step aside, the president of the United States has refused to make good on his own professed policy of regime change in Syria. Barack Obama has ignored both domestic critics of his position on Syria as well as Washington's traditional regional partners clamoring for American leadership. In failing to intervene in the Syrian civil war for humanitarian reasons while also seizing a strategic opportunity to topple Assad, Obama has had to face down even members of his own administration, virtually all of whom, including cabinet officials and some of his closest aides, eventually came to argue for arming the anti-Assad rebels. Although Obama contends that he has on his side the vast majority of a war-weary America, an electorate that loathes the idea of yet another entanglement in the Middle East, the reality is that it was Obama himself who consistently undercut any alternatives. The US public, never eager for foreign adventures in the first place, was simply following the lead of a president who never made the case for a policy that could advance American interests and help save those destined for Assad's meat grinder, without having to land tens of thousands of US troops.

The many apparent turns, nuances, and shifts in the administration's Syria policy—for instance, repeated promises of enhanced military aid to the rebels, the red line drawn over Assad's use of chemical weapons, the threat to strike regime targets after Assad used his unconventional arsenal, and the decision not to—were parts of a messaging campaign intended to further protect Obama's steel-like determination to stay out of the Syrian conflict no matter what. Regardless of what one may think of his policy, the fact that

Obama deflected every argument, entreaty, enticement, and forecast of impending doom to preserve that policy cannot fail to impress. However, history offers conflicting evidence as to whether single-mindedness and obstinacy are necessarily desirable character traits in a man whose job also requires flexibility, the willingness to listen to seasoned advisers, and the ability to change course—in short, the practical talent of democratic politics. He owns his decisions on the Syrian conflict so singly and so starkly that perhaps the judgment on his policy can only be equally absolute: either he was right and kept the United States clear of a prolonged conflict in Syria and built the foundations of a new Middle East; or he was wrong and in ruining Washington's decades-long position in the region ushered in an era of instability whose ripples will reach far past the Persian Gulf littoral and affect all the world.

What is difficult about assessing the president's Syria policy is that there is not much evidence of how Obama sees the Middle East in general and America's role there. Compare Obama's regional strategy, for instance, to that of his predecessor.

Shortly after the 2003 invasion of Iraq, George W. Bush laid out his freedom agenda for the Middle East in a series of speeches that made a clear case for why promoting democracy was not only good for Arab societies but also in the American national interest. In contrast, Obama's speeches, starting with his June 2009 Cairo address, have been vague on specifics. To be sure, his speeches and official statements have touched on various priorities—like Arab-Israeli peace, as he explained in his 2013 address to the UN General Assembly, and Iran's nuclear program—but they lack an integrated vision of the region and America's purpose there. Accordingly, it's been difficult for many observers to discern whether this White House has a coherent Middle East policy or if it is simply improvising on the fly.

However, the Obama administration as a whole has tended to favor communicating with the public in settings less structured than public addresses and official statements. It is in Obama's interviews with the press, as well as information leaked after informal off-the-record briefings with select journalists, where we can find at least some inkling of his grand strategy for the Middle East. The outline started to become clearer in his second presidential term. His goal, as he has explained to David Remnick of the *New Yorker* in January 2013 and Jeffrey Goldberg of Bloomberg News in March 2014, is to create a "geopolitical equilibrium." By balancing traditional American partners like Saudi Arabia and Israel against the Islamic Republic of Iran, Obama hopes to create a new regional security architecture, one ensuring American interests and alleviating the sectarian conflict now ravaging the Middle East, from the deserts of Iraq to the shores of Lebanon. Obama sees the Syrian conflict in the framework of this larger picture.

Whether Obama turns out to be right or wrong, his critics, including this writer, made a fundamental error in their early assessment of his Syria policy. We questioned his ability to read the strategic landscape of the Middle East. For at least two years into the uprising, his opponents—from US senators like John McCain to the Saudi royal family—pounded their heads in frustration. Doesn't he get it? Toppling Assad, as retired Marine Corps General James Mattis put it, "would be the biggest strategic setback for Iran in 25 years."

As it turns out, Obama did see the big picture. Like his many critics, he, too, saw Syria primarily in the larger context of Iran. He refused to take serious action against Assad not only because he saw himself as the president elected to extricate America from Middle Eastern conflict rather than further implicate us, but also because it was central to his concept of US policy in the Middle East.

If Obama's gambit, his big idea about geopolitical equilibrium, and subsequent decision to stay out of Syria turn out to be right, then they will eventually entail a historical reconsideration of much of the American policy establishment's common wisdom. Obama will have been right to believe that the oil-rich Middle East and America's long-standing allies there, from Israel and Egypt to Saudi Arabia and Jordan, were for a number of factors no longer as important as US policy-makers had come to believe over the past half-century. Among other things, with the United States perhaps on the verge of energy independence, it will mean Obama was right to see that the region was still important but no longer vital to American interests, and the US could afford to draw down. And in minimizing the American footprint, Obama will have been right to have bequeathed to the region a new arrangement balancing Washington's traditional Sunni Arab allies in the Persian Gulf against Iran. Although it will continue to be impossible to regard the Syrian civil war as anything but a tragedy, in balancing the Gulf's two great powers, Obama's success here will be to have precluded the possibility of a similar conflict from ever erupting again. If the Middle East was still nothing like Scandinavia, Obama's big idea had nonetheless worked to stabilize it.

If on the other hand Obama turns out to be wrong, then failing to stop Bashar al-Assad will forever stain his historical legacy. It will have been the broad mainstream of the US policy establishment and America's Middle East allies who were right. Sure Obama stood firm, but for what purpose? By allowing the Syrian civil war to drag on and Assad to stay in power, he was idle as Syria's neighbors, including US allies, suffered catastrophic refugee crises, while Iran extended its reach across the Levant. Obama's manifest weakness, underscored by his dealings with Russia, his treatment of allies, and his exertions to shrink America's profile in the region unraveled the American-backed order of the Middle East. Washington's position as a great power and a power broker was established and maintained by generations of Americans—presidents, policy-makers, diplomats, soldiers, educators, business-men, and missionaries—who understood the region not only in terms of the energy resources that made postwar America possible, but also as a testing ground of the country's political, military, historical, and cultural role in the world. What right did Obama have to toss away a national patrimony, and for what purpose?

II: HISTORY'S SEEDS

The seeds of both the Syrian rebellion and the Obama administration's response were planted long before the uprising started. Regarding the former, it's useful to turn to the post–World War I

French mandate, which eventually lead to modern Syria and Lebanon. France's main geopolitical rival in the Middle East, Great Britain, managed its regional holdings largely through the Sunnis, but the French worked through minorities. In Syria, Paris played on minority resentment and anxiety to create a military, security, and intelligence apparatus out of the Alawites and other heterodox Shia sects, like the Ismailis and Druze, long despised by the Sunni urban elite for their "heretical" beliefs and practices. As plans were being drawn for post-mandate Syria, the Alawites petitioned French authorities for their own state and begged not "to be joined to Syria for it is a Sunni state and Sunnis consider them unbelievers," as a letter from Alawite notables to the French prime minister explained. The "hatred and fanaticism embedded in the hearts of the Arab Muslims against everything that is non-Muslim," the letter went on, would expose the Alawites to "annihilation."

There were theological sources for Sunni triumphalism, vigorously expressed, for instance, by the fourteenth-century Hanbali cleric Ibn

Taymiyya, a major influence on the Salafi-jihadi movement. He wrote that war against and punishment of the Alawites "are among the greatest of pious deeds and the most important obligation." And there were also class and cultural factors dividing the Sunnis and Alawites. In his 2012 book *The Syrian Rebellion,* the great historian of the modern Middle East Fouad Ajami recalls that, "In my boyhood in Beirut, there were countless Alawi servants, young girls delivered into families with means to feed the girls' families back home." The Sunnis regarded these inhabitants of the coastal mountain range as peasants—"a heterodox sect of peasants," writes Ajami, who "had conquered their homeland." Damascus had been the capital of the historical Sunni Arab heartland dating to the seventh Umayyad caliphate (661–750 CE).

In a sense, the March 2011 uprising was simply another phase in a prolonged conflict that started when a minority sect came to rule the country's, and the region's, Sunni Arab majority. When Hafez al-Assad became president in 1970, replacing Syria's first Alawite ruler Salah Jadid who had come to power in 1966, he met Sunni resentment with punishing resolve during the course of a Muslim Brotherhood-led insurgency that began shortly after Syria's 1976 invasion of Lebanon. Assad's counterinsurgency culminated in the massacre at Hama, a Brotherhood stronghold where his men killed between 10,000 and 40,000 people.

Bashar al-Assad used the history of Sunni-Alawite enmity as the cornerstone of a strategic messaging campaign that resonated in a post-9/11 America reeling from the attacks on the World Trade Center and Pentagon. We share the same enemy, Assad told the Bush White House—Sunni extremists, Al Qaeda. What Assad's narrative elided was that sometimes the regime in Damascus would team up with Al Qaeda, most spectacularly against the Americans themselves. And it is here where the roots of the Obama administration's response to the Syrian conflict are intertwined with those of the anti-Assad rebellion.

For some time after 9/11, the Assad regime seemed to cooperate with Washington, reportedly sharing intelligence and accepting detainees for extraordinary rendition. The relationship began to sour with the US-led invasion of Iraq in 2003, which both Syria and Iran initially saw as an existential threat drawn up to their borders. Both fought back in their customary fashion, through terrorist cutouts, with the Iranians sponsoring mostly Shia militants and the Syrians offering their services to Sunni fighters. Damascus International Airport became a key transit hub for foreign jihadists, who were then bused by Syrian intelligence to the Iraq border where they took up arms against US troops and their Iraqi allies.

American officials, civilian and military, warned the Syrians on this and other matters, but the regime turned a deaf ear, perhaps assuming the Americans weren't serious, and even if they were Assad had more pressing worries. He was concerned that the Sunni majority he ruled would draw a dangerous conclusion from the White House's project next door. If the Americans were largely driven by a post-9/11 animus toward the Sunnis that saw Saddam Hussein as the most convenient way to teach the Arabs a lesson, the freedom agenda still spelled trouble for a minority Alawite regime. Syria's Sunni community could hardly fail to notice that if democracy meant that power fell to the country's Shia majority in Iraq, in Syria it would mean the rightful restoration of Sunni sovereignty in the beating heart of Arabism and, Assad feared, the inevitable satisfaction of a vendetta against the Alawites.

Assad continued his proxy war in Iraq to prevent regime change and carnage at home by showing Syrians that the Americans' so-called democracy was nothing but sectarian slaughter. He ignored the Americans because this mighty foreign power was also fickle and always had a soft spot for Damascus.

III: THE DEVIL WE KNOW

Among Washington's permanent bureaucracy in the State Department and the intelligence community, Syria has long enjoyed the role of a troubled prodigal child. This perspective on the Damascus regime was the source of much of the criticism of George W. Bush's Syria policy. Former American policy-makers, like those who authored the 2006 Baker-Hamilton Iraq Study Group report advising the Bush administration to reach out to all the regional stakeholders, just couldn't see the wisdom in isolating Assad rather than making him part of the solution. And when the Syrian uprising broke out in 2011, this same indulgent view would earn Assad some support in Washington—sure he's a tyrant, but he's the devil we know, and we could trust his father, a man who kept his word. The autobiographical accounts of American diplomats who held Hafez al-Assad in the highest esteem as a statesman, even as they abased themselves at his feet and endured countless humiliations at his hands, were no doubt part of his son's calculations regarding Iraq. The Americans can blow as much smoke as much as they like, the younger Assad may have assumed, but they won't do a damn thing. It was only after Assad was suspected of killing former Lebanese Prime Minister Rafik Hariri along with 22 others in a massive car bombing in Beirut on February 14, 2005, that Bush decided he'd had enough and withdrew the US ambassador to Damascus.

The Hariri murder was one of the contributing factors leading to the uprising in Syria six years later. Hafez al-Assad had alternately repressed and co-opted Syria's Sunni community, typically through Sunni regime figures who held, in name at least, important posts, like vice president, foreign minister, and defense minister. But his son Bashar shrunk the regime so that it excluded all but immediate family members, the Assads and his cousins on his mother's side, the Makhloufs. He made no room for his father's Sunnis and had no patience for those on the Lebanese side of the border who he believed had taken sides against him. Hariri was expendable, Assad believed, and his public execution would serve as an example.

If, in a less impulsive moment, Assad might have been able to foresee the angry American and French responses to the Hariri assassination, it's unlikely he imagined that the lesson he intended to teach his subjects in the Levant had the opposite effect. From the Sunni point of view, it wasn't enough for Assad to rule over the Sunnis and repress them in Syria, but even the blood of major Sunni leaders in Lebanon, where under Hafez they had been allowed a certain degree of independence, was licit. Assad had reopened the regime's war against Sunnis in the most public fashion possible.

Another seedling of the 2011 uprising was the Iraq war. At the time, I was living in Beirut and visited Damascus frequently. During one trip I spoke with a local merchant who insisted that if a similar sectarian conflict were to erupt in Syria it would be much worse, for the Syrians were that much more ferocious and the Sunnis, he suggested, that much more resentful. I now believe that he was correct. If the bloodshed is not yet worse than Iraq, it is heading there quickly. There are perhaps already as many casualties as there were during Lebanon's fifteen-year civil war, which claimed 150,000 lives. As with the Hariri assassination, here was another pattern Assad misjudged. If he thought the chaos he'd helped cultivate in Iraq would deter Syrian Sunnis from seeking a similar dispensation, it seems the violence only steeled them for the bloody work necessary to bring down a tyrant. By the time the Arab Spring uprisings in Tunisia,

Egypt, Libya, and Bahrain broke out in the winter of 2010–11, Syria was primed.

As Bush White House officials would later confess, the administration's policy of isolating Assad came up short. To be sure, it was gratifying that for a brief period anyway the leader of the free world treated the regime as the murderous organized crime family it is, and not as a special case to be indulged and its bloody actions ignored. But leaving Assad out in the cold had not changed his behavior. Indeed, even before the 2008 presidential campaigns, when various nominees argued over engaging rogue regimes like Assad's, as well as Tehran, Washington moved toward rapprochement with Damascus. In the fall of 2007, Secretary of State Condoleezza Rice invited the Syrians to attend a Middle East peace conference in Annapolis, MD. By the time Barack Obama took office in January 2009, Syria was rehabilitated and restored to its traditional role in American Middle East policy as a stubborn but nonetheless central player in the region.

In 2010, the administration returned an ambassador to Syria, Robert Ford, but it was John Kerry, then chairman of the Senate Committee on Foreign Relations, who seemed to be running point. He traveled to Damascus several times and spoke highly of the man he described as a reformer and moderate. If the infamous picture of then-Senator Kerry and his wife, Teresa, dining out in Damascus with Bashar and Asma al-Assad may now cause the current secretary of state some embarrassment, it was an open secret in Washington that the Kerrys were captivated by the "Westernized" Syrian president and his stylish first lady.

As the new White House saw it early on, Syria was key to Obama's two chief Middle East initiatives, the peace process and engaging Iran diplomatically in order to halt its march toward the bomb. Obama believed that the two were linked, and Syria was part of the equation. "If we've gotten an Israeli-Palestinian peace deal," he said in 2008, "maybe at the same time peeling Syria out of the Iranian orbit, that makes it easier to isolate Iran so that they have a tougher time developing a nuclear weapon."

The purpose of engaging Syria was to drive a wedge between Damascus and its strategic ally. If the plan was fanciful, it's nonetheless worth noting that this tactic represents a very different view of how the US should treat the Syria-Iran relationship than the one that would later determine Obama's policy on the Syrian civil war. In the former instance, he wanted to isolate and thereby weaken Iran. In the latter, the White House's actions are evidence it believed that any efforts to bring down Iran's only client in the Arab state system would alienate a regime with which Obama was keen to strike a bargain.

Perhaps the template for the second approach was set in the aftermath of Iran's June 2009 elections. Critics wondered why the White House balked at publicly supporting the protest movement that took to the streets over the likely fraudulent vote count that returned Mahmoud Ahmadinejad to the presidency. But, as one former Obama administration official explained to the *New Yorker,* "We were still trying to engage the Iranian government, and we did not want to do anything that made us side with the protesters."

Coming out early with strong support for Iran's Green Movement might have threatened the regime's prestige and demonstrated the strength of Washington's soft power, an instrument the administration professes to value. But Obama didn't want to aggravate the Iranians. For the same reason, he resisted early on imposing sanctions on the clerical regime, and only congressional pressure forced his hand. When the Senate put forth another sanctions bill in 2014, Obama threatened to veto it.

He saw the Syrian conflict from the same perspective. According to press reports, Vice President Joe Biden's national security adviser Jake Sullivan was leading the American side in secret negotiations with Iran by July 2012. In other words, since at least then and perhaps much earlier, Obama likely saw the Syrian conflict simply in light of Iran talks.

To be sure, helping to topple Assad would have struck a severe blow to the Iranians by eliminating a strategic partner that among other things served as their supply line to Hezbollah. Syria is Iran's 35th province, a strategic province for us, said one senior Iranian cleric in the winter of 2013. "If the enemy attacks us and wants to take either Syria or Khuzestan, the priority for us is to keep Syria. . . . If we keep Syria, we can get Khuzestan back, too; but if we lose Syria, we cannot keep Tehran."

Like his critics, Obama understood the strategic relationship between Tehran and Damascus, but rather than leverage against the regime he sought an accommodation with it. His assessment of Tehran's psychological profile warned him against pressuring the Iranians on a strategically vital issue like Syria. His kid-glove approach to Iran aligns him with the view that the primary reason Tehran wants a nuclear weapons program is as insurance against regime change. On this line of thinking, acquiring the bomb will serve to normalize an anxiety-ridden, perhaps paranoid, ruling order and turn it into a more or less responsible actor. Consequently, it would be at cross-purposes to try to weaken the regime for the purposes of negotiating over a nuclear weapons program that it seeks precisely because it feels vulnerable. Obama wanted to soothe the Iranians, not antagonize them further—he didn't just want to get them to the table and stop their nuclear weapons program, he also wanted to put an end to the 35-year-long hostilities with the Islamic Republic and turn it into a partner.

Historical reconciliation with Tehran is one of the collective dreams of the American foreign policy establishment, as is Palestinian-Israeli peace, which in the imagination of many policy elites is the golden key that unlocks every other seemingly intractable problem in the region. Failing at the peace process halfway through his first term further focused Obama's attention on Iran. It was a positive development that he no longer understood the entire Middle East simply as an outgrowth of the "core" conflict between Arabs and Palestinians, but this also left him without the sort of overarching theoretical apparatus that seems to stir his intellect and emotions. "I am comfortable with complexity," Obama once told a journalist. He likes systems and networks, and to find causes, connections, and genealogies, the larger relationships between things that make the world make sense. Yes, there are discrete entities in the world, ideas, and policies that have no obvious connection to other things, but these aren't as interesting. The next big idea after the peace process was an idea about Iran.

Through various journalists whom Obama is known to use as sounding boards, the president began to drop hints about his grand strategy for the Middle East toward the end of 2013. For instance, *Washington Post* columnist David Ignatius wrote in October that, "The United States will be stronger if it can create a new framework for security in the Middle East that involves Iran and defuses the Sunni-Shiite sectarian conflict threatening the region."

Of course, this framework isn't new at all, but is rather based on the pre-1979 twin-pillar policy, which saw Saudi Arabia and Iran as the cornerstones of Washington's security architecture in the Persian Gulf. What made the strategy unworkable now was simply the fact that Iran under the shah was a US ally, and the clerical regime has treated America as an enemy ever since the Islamic Revolution.

American policy-makers are right to recognize that sectarianism is a problem throughout the region. However, it is an error of the first order for them to understand or describe the region in those terms. Their job is to maintain and advance American interests and shape policy according to allies and adversaries, not Sunnis and Shiites, both of which may and do fall into either category. The most salient issue then for American policy-makers isn't sectarian conflict, which is beyond their power to defuse in the first place, but that Saudi Arabia, the Gulf's Sunni Arab superpower, is still a part of the American regional order, and Iran, the Shia Persian superpower, is a revolutionary regime.

The problematic nature of Iran's behavior is not lost on Obama. As he told David Remnick of the *New Yorker* in January 2014, "If we were able to get Iran to operate in a responsible fashion— not funding terrorist organizations, not trying to stir up sectarian discontent in other countries, and not developing a nuclear weapon—you could see an equilibrium."

The question is, how do you do that? Or more basically, should American policy-makers even concern themselves with that question? Or rather should they accept the nature of the regime for what it is and, instead of trying to turn an adversary of 35 years into a "responsible" regional security partner, deal with it accordingly?

As Obama explained in the January *New Yorker* article, he sees a "geopolitical equilibrium . . . 'developing between Sunni, or predominantly Sunni, Gulf states and Iran in which there's competition, perhaps suspicion, but not an active or proxy warfare.'" Competition and even conflicts will still exist in the region, he continued, but it's "contained, it is expressed in ways that don't exact such an enormous toll on the countries involved, and that allow us to work with functioning states to prevent extremists from emerging there."

This is the language of the academy, more specifically of realism, an international relations theory holding that all states are fundamentally rational insofar as they are predisposed to advance their national interest. Thus, the belief systems and ideological convictions that allegedly motivate them are immaterial. For Obama, the issue with Iran is not in its nature, but in its conduct, which is irresponsible. From the realist perspective, it is nonsense to argue, for instance, that the actions the Iranian regime takes—its support for terrorism, etc.—is how this ruling order manifests its particular nature in the world. Regimes don't have natures, just interests, which is why, for example, from the realist perspective the debate over whether or not the regime is rational and therefore susceptible to nuclear deterrence should it acquire the bomb is a waste of time. Of course, the Iranians are rational—no regime is irrational, insofar as no ruling order seeks its own end. On this count at least the realists are right. What they are missing, however, is that history is nothing but the record of fallen nations, lost tribes, and forgotten peoples who have miscalculated their own ability to project power and the willingness of their adversaries to challenge them.

The problem with realism is that it is a worldview lacking the tragic sense or an understanding of human history that sees, as the ancient Greeks did, character as destiny. People do what they do because they can't help themselves; it's in their nature. And you can't change the behavior of regimes because they can't change it themselves. Obama discounts the Iranian regime's ideological content, because, while he acknowledges its bad behavior, in the end it's a "functioning state"—and therefore manageable through the various instruments that other states use to engage or deter their peers. If international conferences and multilateral agreements fail, you can always, as a last resort, deploy your financial, security, and military institutions against theirs. As Obama told journalist Jeffrey Goldberg, "If you look at Iranian behavior, they are strategic, and they're not impulsive. They have a worldview, and they see their interests, and they respond to costs and benefits."

That is not how Obama sees non-state actors. Accordingly, for the Obama administration the key regional threat wasn't the Islamic Republic's nuclear program, or Iranian expansionism, but Al Qaeda. How could you deter, never mind diplomatically engage, lone wolves, non-state actors lacking the political, diplomatic, and security institutions that make states part of the international state system? The only answer for Al Qaeda is drone strikes, Special Forces raids, and clandestine operations.

The White House's Syria policy underscored those strategic priorities. As outgoing CIA Deputy

Director Michael Morell explained to the *Wall Street Journal* in the summer of 2013, the intelligence community believed that the number one threat to US national interests was a failed state in Syria that would fall into the hands of Al Qaeda. This is why the administration insisted on preserving Syria's state institutions, regardless of Assad's fate. To be sure, Obama wanted to avoid a repeat of the carnage that followed the Bush administration's de-Baathification policy, but there was a larger issue at stake.

IV: THE JIHADIST ALIBI

From the White House's perspective, failed states are breeding grounds for terrorism—or more specifically, terrorism that can't be deterred. If Sunni terrorism is most often an index of the weakness of Sunni-majority states and their inability to control their jihadist hordes, Iranian-backed terrorism is a token of the strength and coherence of the regime in Tehran. From this point of view, if you can make a deal with the Iranians, you can take Hezbollah off the board;

there's no similar command and control for Al Qaeda.

However, the fact that the main Al Qaeda affiliates operating in Syria—Jabhat al-Nusra and the Islamic State in Iraq and Syria—are engaged not only in a bloody war against the regime and Assad's allied forces, but also against other rebel units and sometimes even themselves, suggests both operational and strategic disarray. The notion that Al Qaeda, rather than Iran, a coherent nation-state building a nuclear bomb, constitutes the greatest threat to American citizens at home is comprehensible only in the context of the administration's larger theoretical framework. For Obama, Iran isn't the problem; rather, Iran is the key to the solution. Bringing Tehran into a regional security architecture alongside America's traditional Arab allies in the Persian Gulf would create a new balance of power, where there would still be competition, and perhaps some conflict, but not at the same levels, since it would neutralize them and their proxies, Al Qaeda for the Sunnis, and for Iran, Hezbollah.

As one administration official told the *New York Times* in October 2013, White House chief of staff Denis McDonough argued against backing the Syrian rebels to topple Assad for just this reason: a prolonged conflict between Al Qaeda and Hezbollah was good for American interests. From this perspective, the best outcome was to let the two sides bleed each other indefinitely while the US stayed on the sidelines. This reading was apparently oblivious to the fact that the Middle East is more than Al Qaeda and Hezbollah. After all, the civil war threatens to destabilize American allies on Syria's borders, while the sectarian conflict spreads from Baghdad to Beirut.

In order to deflect criticism of Obama's passive and often contradictory Syria policy, the administration waged a formidable public messaging campaign that picked up on a variety of themes, some of which were re-used repeatedly, while others were tweaked slightly or simply dropped as events required.

The White House wasn't moving against Assad as it had with Libyan ruler Muammar el-Qaddafi, Secretary of State Hillary Clinton reasoned early on, because Assad was not using planes to shoot his opposition like Qaddafi did. Clinton's implicit red line on the use of fixed-wing aircraft was quietly dropped after Assad began to strafe and bomb civilian areas.

Administration officials leaked to the press that the Israelis had warned against toppling the devil they knew. The story may have served to ward off criticism from some of America's Arab allies—blaming Israel was a tactic pulled out of the Arab regime playbook—but it was false. Israel's ambassador to Washington Michael Oren wrote letters to the *Wall Street Journal* on two occasions to correct the record—"I emphatically denied this the first time and categorically deny it again," wrote Oren. "Israel has expressed no such concerns. Allied with Iran, Mr. Assad has helped supply 55,000 rockets to Hezbollah and 10,000 to Hamas, very likely established a clandestine nuclear arms program and profoundly destabilized the region." He concluded, "The violence he has unleashed on his own people demonstrating for freedoms confirms Israel's fears that the devil we know in Syria is worse than the devil we don't." By May 2011 Israel's top officials—the prime minister, defense minister, foreign minister, and president—had stated publicly that they were eager to see Assad gone, three months before Obama did.

When the opposition picked up weapons in self-defense, the administration said it didn't know who the rebels were and was reluctant to furnish them with arms that might wind up being used against US allies, like Israel. And the White House didn't need to arm the rebels anyway, officials argued, because Assad's downfall was a matter of when, not if. He's a dead man walking, said one of the administration's Syria hands.

As the death toll mounted, US lawmakers like Senators John McCain and Lindsey Graham and former Senator Joe Lieberman called for international airpower, led by the US, to create a no-fly zone, or a buffer zone, offering civilians some sort of refuge from the regime's depredations. Pentagon officials explained this wasn't as easy as it sounded—the Syrians had serious Russian-made air defense systems that, to hear then-Secretary of Defense Leon Panetta and Chairman of the Joint Chiefs of Staff General Martin Dempsey tell it, were virtually impregnable. McCain bristled. "We spend almost

$1 trillion a year on the military," he told CNN. "And we can't take out air defenses of Syria? That is a horrific waste of the taxpayers' dollars."

The debate over Syrian air defenses brings to mind Karfan, the lead character of the *Syria Exposed* blog, which lasted only a brief time in the mid-2000s, when the freedom agenda was still a going concern in the Middle East and a Syrian blogger might dream of the main chance that the Iraqis and Lebanese had seized to try to win their freedoms. The blog's conceit was that its English-language author was a friend of Karfan and relayed his thoughts, ideas, and memories, like those of his time in the Syrian army.

"Back when Karfan was forced to serve his country and waste two years of his already useless life in the army, he was assigned to a radar unit in Lebanon. . . . Service at a radar station was both the most useless and most dangerous service in the Syrian Army. They were not allowed to ever turn on those junk backward radars the Russians had bullied Syria into buying. If they operate them, the Israelis would detect their location, send missiles and blow the whole thing up. You cannot think of any more useless way to spend a year and a half of your life: you have to sit inside a dead piece of junk that is supposed to detect enemy's airlines, but you cannot turn it on because if you do, it would be blown away, with you in it of course." The concern, Karfan explained, was that a commanding officer would order them to turn on the radars. "Every one there knew what would happen then," said Karfan. "They code named it: The Suicide Order."

Karfan's Kafkaesque accounts of life in a modern Arab nationalist police state puts the administration's claims regarding Syrian air defense systems in their proper context. More importantly, in reading his blog it was possible years before the rebellion started to sense the growing frustration and anger of a young Syrian middle-class that deserved more than the token reforms implemented by the young Syrian president to impress Western policy-makers. Karfan's was a harbinger of the uprising's democratic voice, nearly half a decade before the uprising itself, a voice that would be drowned out by the many thousands of Syrians fed through the buzz saw of Assad's killing machine. In the meantime, the

White House continued manufacturing justifications for doing nothing so as to not upset the Iranians.

Indeed, according to another White House talking point at the time, backing Assad is hurting Iran and consuming its financial resources. Syria, so went the common wisdom, is Iran's Vietnam. Maybe so, but Tehran continued to task Hezbollah and various Iraqi militias to support Assad's depleted military and paramilitary forces because the Iranians, contrary to the claims of the Obama administration, believed that there was indeed a military solution—win. One of the White House's political solutions was the Arab League initiative to broker a cease-fire—the only game in town, said Obama aides. And then the White House claimed that the Russians were the only game in town, even though they'd repeatedly vetoed resolutions against Assad at the UN Security Council and showed no sign of abandoning their client in Damascus.

The White House publicly chided the opposition's political leadership, which it found fragmented and fractious. And arming the military leadership, said other administration officials, would only make things worse. With the regime's campaign of sectarian cleansing targeting several towns and neighborhoods abutting Alawite districts, Assad had seeded blood debts throughout the country. The conclusion that White House aides and various press surrogates drew from Assad's wanton slaughter of Sunnis was that the Alawites and other minorities needed to be protected when the Sunnis came for payback.

This message struck home with a number of American policy-makers like Senator Rand Paul and pundits on the right who professed concern for the fate of Syria's Christian community without apparently giving much thought to the scores of Sunnis that Assad and his allies had crushed like insects. Why Paul and others argued that the Christians and their clerics who'd publicly cheered Assad's atrocities warranted special protection probably had little to do with Christian charity or fellow sentiment. The Gospels, after all, offer no example of Christ petitioning Pilate to decimate other sects so that his flock may thrive. Rather, Paul's advocacy suggested that it wasn't so much war that Americans were tired of—rather, they were tired of Muslims.

The contempt expressed in some quarters showed that there was only a thin line between isolationism and bigotry. "Let Allah sort it out," said Sarah Palin, which was in fact only the more conspicuously vicious version of chief of staff McDonough's belief that it was good for America if Hezbollah and Al Qaeda killed each other. It seems never to have occurred, or perhaps never to have mattered, to the "pity they both can't lose" school that there were millions of civilians caught in the cross fire.

The notion that minorities needed to be protected from Sunnis synchronized almost seamlessly with Assad's own strategic communications campaign. For the past decade, he'd been telling anyone who would listen that he and the Americans shared the same mortal enemy— Al Qaeda. No one paid much mind back then, even when he was running his anti-Sunni, anti-Saudi disinformation campaign through the *New Yorker* journalist Seymour Hersh, who dutifully relayed regime talking points in his articles and television interviews; but now, Assad hit pay dirt. Nearly a year after the uprising began, the White House had finally discovered who the opposition was—Al Qaeda. In December 2012, the administration designated Jabhat al-Nusra as a foreign terrorist organization. The Syrian opposition was baffled that the White House went after one of the most effective rebel units when the Americans had disdained arming the Free Syrian Army, but the opposition noted that it dovetailed nicely with Assad's propaganda. He'd been saying since the beginning of the uprising that his war wasn't against fellow Syrians, but rather against terrorists, Al Qaeda.

There is no doubt that Sunni extremists, including foreign fighters, came to play a major role in the war. In certain parts of the country, especially near the Turkish border, Al Qaeda affiliates hold large pieces of territory where their atrocities, against townsfolk as well as regime sympathizers, are well-known. But the notion that the majority of rebel units are Al Qaeda is absurd. Indeed, it's not even clear that all the Islamists are actually Islamists. Without Western support, many Syrian fighters flocked to the groups that could offer money and arms, much of it coming from private donors in the Gulf states. Some rebel fighters grew long beards and shouted Islamist slogans out of conviction, and others simply because doing so persuaded Gulf billionaires to keep the spigot on even as the Americans refused to arm them.

John Kerry acknowledged in a hearing on Capitol Hill that there were plenty of non-Al Qaeda units in the Free Syrian Army worthy of American support. But, as other administration officials leaked to the press, they weren't as strong as the Al Qaeda groups. According to the White House, it came down to a choice between Assad and Al Qaeda's project to turn Syria into an Islamic emirate exporting terror around the world. Setting up a no-fly zone would make America Al Qaeda's air force. It was Assad's own messaging campaign—Al Qaeda or me—that became the White House's most effective theme to rationalize its policy choice, its decision not to arm the rebels. Who in their right mind would argue for enabling the engineers of 9/11?

To be sure, there was reason for Americans to be wary of supporting the anti-Assad opposition.

Over the past decade, the United States brought down or helped to bring down four Arab dictators, and with little Arab gratitude for the effort, especially for the sacrifices made by the US armed forces, thousands killed and tens of thousands wounded, so that Iraqis could vote in free and fair elections and live without fear of being dragged off by Saddam's security forces. The Syrian opposition had a special problem in that over forty years very few Syrians had ever publicly opposed the Assad regime's policies when it was killing not only Israelis and Americans, but also other Arabs, like Lebanese, Jordanians, and Palestinians. Without accounting for their years of silence while the Assad regime hunted others, it would be difficult for the political opposition to plan the kind of inclusive Syria it often talked about in public forums. And without any public soul-searching it would be hard to win much support from an American public whose president's chief Middle East initiative compelled him to undercut any support for the opposition.

Still, Obama was surrounded in his own White House by aides and cabinet officials who argued for arming the rebels. In Obama's first term, Clinton, Panetta, and Dempsey all made it clear that they were on board with CIA Director David Petraeus's proposal to arm carefully vetted Free Syrian Army units, a plan the president shot down. Obama then loaded his next cabinet with policy-makers unlikely to urge him to get tougher on Assad. His new national security principals had all left a public record of their desire to extend a friendly hand to either Assad (Kerry and Defense Secretary Chuck Hagel), Iran (Hagel and CIA Director John Brennan) or Hezbollah (Brennan). But Kerry reportedly argued for strikes on Syrian airfields. More significantly, according to a *New York Times* article in October 2013, almost every official who had previously rejected arming the rebels was now in favor of it, including new national security adviser Susan Rice as well as her predecessor, and one of Obama's key political operatives, Thomas Donilon.

It wasn't just McCain-style Republicans and other hawks who believed that arming a proxy force to battle a key adversary comported with a Washington tradition at least as old as the Cold War. There was a broad US foreign policy consensus about backing the rebels on behalf of the national interest to topple an Iranian ally that held even in the Obama administration. The problem, as the *Times* explained, was that the two administration figures swimming against the mainstream were chief of staff McDonough and the president himself.

As one official present at meetings in which Syria policy was discussed told the *New York Times,* Obama "often appeared impatient or disengaged while listening to the debate, sometimes scrolling through messages on his BlackBerry or slouching and chewing gum." The reason why the president seemed absent was perhaps lost on most of his staffers. It became apparent only when press reports explained that administration envoys had been engaged in secret talks with Tehran since at least July 2012. As far as Obama was concerned, the internal White House debate on Syria was just pantomime— the decision against arming the Free Syrian Army had already been made. Obama wasn't going to drive the Iranians away with an active policy to topple Assad, and that policy choice wasn't going to be affected by any new facts on the ground, even the use of chemical weapons.

Obama had first drawn his red line against the use of chemical weapons in August 2012. "That would change my calculations significantly," he explained. Assad's unconventional arsenal is "an issue that doesn't just concern Syria. It concerns our close allies in the region, including Israel." The idea that Assad might deploy chemical weapons against his neighbors, especially Israel, was nonsense since he feared that Israeli retaliation would bring the house down on his head. The chemical weapons arsenal was his insurance policy. In the event that the regime was eventually forced out of Damascus, it would need to cover its retreat and defend its position in the historical Alawite homeland along the coastal mountain range—and it needed chemical weapons for both. The real danger then was that Assad would turn his arsenal on the rebels as well as their civilian base in the Sunni community to show that he was more than willing to use it. Even as the regime claimed that it would use chemical weapons only in case of "external aggression" and never against civilians, from the very beginning of the uprising Assad had described the Sunni opposition as foreign terrorists in a propaganda campaign, which the White House carelessly abetted.

There were frequent rumors that the regime had used chemical weapons, and in April 2013 the White House released a letter explaining that the US "intelligence community does assess with varying degrees of confidence that the Syrian regime has used chemical weapons on a small scale in Syria, specially the chemical agent Sarin." Two months later the administration announced that American intelligence now had a level of high confidence in its assessment. Accordingly, to enforce the president's red line, the administration declared it was augmenting its assistance to the rebels.

McCain went to the Senate floor and said Obama "will announce that we will be assisting the Syrian rebels by providing them with weapons and other assistance. I applaud the president's decision." Shortly after, McCain retracted his remarks. The president, he said, "has not made the final decision on arming."

The confusion grew. The official responsible for rolling out what the administration was selling as a new policy was Ben Rhodes, deputy national security adviser for strategic communications and an Obama confidante. His phone call with reporters on June 13 hardly helped clarify matters. Journalists repeatedly pressed to find out what kind of aid the administration had in mind, if it was just more nonlethal military assistance, like vehicles and night-vision goggles, that the White House had previously promised and failed to deliver, or if Obama was really going to arm the rebels. "We're just not going to be able to lay out an inventory of what exactly falls under the scope of that assistance," Rhodes answered evasively.

Obama himself provided no more insight when in an appearance on the *Charlie Rose* show, the commander in chief told his host, "I've said I'm ramping up support for both the political and military opposition. I've not specified exactly what we're doing, and I won't do so on this show." The sole confirmation the administration was sending arms came from press reports sourced only to anonymous officials who because they went unnamed had no reason to fear that their credibility was on the line if their information proved inaccurate or false.

The key to understanding what transpired in June—whether the White House actually meant to arm the Syrian opposition or if Obama just wanted to create the impression that he was enforcing his red line—was in the rollout. If the administration had really intended to send weapons, then that would have constituted a significant shift in policy. Since it was Obama's red line that Assad had crossed, the president himself might have made an official statement, or at least the national security adviser or some other cabinet official responsible for policy decisions should have stepped forward. Instead, it was given to a deputy inside Obama's inner circle who handles strategic communications. There was no change in policy; it was just more messaging. Subsequent press reports and interviews with rebel commanders over the next few months showed the White House was not in fact sending arms.

It's not clear that Assad was ever concerned Obama would enforce his red line. Various intelligence assessments found the regime had used chemical weapons many times after Obama's admonition. Even if Assad didn't know anything about the administration's ongoing secret talks with Iran, his and his father's past experiences with American policy-makers showed that a lot of their tough talk was empty bluster. Besides, there were no longer the 150,000 US troops on his Iraq border whose presence, and Bush's unpredictable temperament, forced him to withdraw his own troops from Lebanon in 2005, two months after the Hariri assassination. Instead, there were rebel forces that had held key suburbs of Damascus for over a year. The regime needed to retake those neighborhoods overlooking the Damascus-Homs highway, one of the regime's main communications lines, and a corridor a little farther northeast leading to Dumayr, an airport where Assad's allied forces are supplied by direct flights from Iran. In August, the regime launched a chemical weapons attack on this region, targeting in particular East Ghouta.

When news broke of the attack, and the hundreds of casualties it caused, it was two years after Obama had first called on Assad to step aside and a year after he first drew his red line. Assad had both defied Obama and called his bluff. White House press briefings after the incident showed a president who was angry, decisive, determined to punish Assad, and yet circumspect. "I have gotten options from our military, had extensive discussions with my national security team," Obama said on the PBS *NewsHour*, explaining that he might yet choose not to pull the trigger. "I've not made a decision," he said.

But the decision had already been made when the president chose to make the Syrian conflict a subset of his Iran policy.

White House staffers, Obama allies, and a cooperative press corps praised the president's judiciousness when he decided to refer the matter to Congress for an authorization of military force. However, the administration's messaging campaign—the opposition was all Al Qaeda, tens of thousands of US troops on the ground might not change the balance of power, the American people were war-weary—had virtually ensured Obama would lose an authorization he never needed in the first place.

Russian President Vladimir Putin's last-minute offer to team up with the White House to rid Assad of his chemical weapons arsenal extricated Obama from the corner he'd backed himself into, but at a huge cost to American and his own personal prestige. Putin had scored off of Obama's real liability, his vanity. Obama, Putin saw, always needs to look good. He will embrace defeat so long as he can still imagine himself triumphant. After pushing Obama around for five years, with the Russian initiative Putin made himself the indispensable power in the Middle East.

Maybe none of that mattered to Obama. After all, his task was to lead America out of the region, not further in. In place of the American-backed order of the region, privileging and protecting traditional allies from Saudi Arabia to Israel, he was building a new security architecture that could stand without Washington's active support. The important thing with Syria was to stay out of the war, to keep America free from the conflict and the Iranians at the table. After all, the Syrian civil war was only a symptom of the region's larger problems, which could be solved, or at least attenuated, if he had a deal with Iran. If critics argued that Putin's intervention made Obama look weak, it allowed him to defend his big idea, his anatomy of a new Middle East.

After the White House and the rest of the P5-plus-1 struck an interim deal with Iran in November 2013 over the regime's nuclear weapons program, America's regional partners complained that the White House was tilting against them and toward the Iranian-led axis of resistance. And indeed, the Russian initiative to rid Assad of his chemical weapons arsenal turned Assad into an American partner. With the tacit support of the White House now, as well as the explicit backing of Iran and Russia, Assad isn't going anywhere—unless he's killed by the opposition. Given the scale of the atrocities the regime has already committed without eliciting any American reprisal, it's hard to imagine what, short of a chemical weapons attack on New York City, would compel the administration to intervene and bring down Assad and thereby make good on a policy that some in the administration reportedly wish the president had never spoken in August 2011 or ever.

Perhaps the next White House will see things differently, but the Syrian civil war, which will almost certainly burn hot the next three years and longer, will also have changed by then. More foreign fighters will pour in, and more Syrian civilians will leave to seek refuge in numbers that are likely to pose serious problems, including political instability and violence, for neighboring countries as well as elsewhere, including Europe and North America. There will be more death, too, in Syria as well as other states where the Iranians have staked an interest, especially Lebanon and Iraq. It's quite possible that an entire generation, reaching from Beirut to Baghdad, will either be lost to war or have their lives, ideas, and beliefs shaped by it.

The next White House will have to deal with the region that this one will hand off to it—more violence, allies betrayed, adversaries emboldened, and Iran almost certainly on the verge of a nuclear breakout that will further destabilize a vitally strategic region that most of the industrialized

world, including major American trading partners, depend on to fulfill their energy needs. It
will come back to us, too. In time Americans
will come to understand that Obama's diminish-
ment of American power means their diminish-
ment, too.

ABOUT THE AUTHOR

LEE SMITH is a senior editor at *the Weekly Standard* and a senior fellow at the Hudson Institute in Washington, DC. He also writes a regular column, "Agents of Influence," about US foreign policy and the Middle East, for *Tablet Magazine;* he has also written extensively on Arab and Islamic affairs, contributing articles to, among other publications, the *New York Times,* the *Wall Street Journal, TIME,* Slate.com, and *Wired.* His book, *The Strong Horse: Power, Politics, and the Clash of Arab Civilizations,* was published in January 2010 by Doubleday. Smith has been a guest commentator on radio and television, including CNN, Fox News, and National Public Radio.

Smith has a BA from George Washington University, where he received awards in English and Latin. He received the Sage Graduate School Fellowship at Cornell University and studied Arabic at the American University in Cairo and the Université Saint-Joseph in Beirut.

HERBERT AND JANE DWIGHT
WORKING GROUP ON
ISLAMISM AND THE
INTERNATIONAL ORDER

The Herbert and Jane Dwight Working Group on Islamism and the International Order seeks to engage in the task of reversing Islamic radicalism through reforming and strengthening the legitimate role of the state across the entire Muslim world. Efforts will draw on the intellectual resources of an array of scholars and practitioners from within the United States and abroad, to foster the pursuit of modernity, human flourishing, and the rule of law and reason in Islamic lands—developments that are critical to the very order of the international system.

The Working Group is cochaired by Hoover fellows Fouad Ajami and Charles Hill, with an active participation by Hoover Institution Director John Raisian. Current core membership includes Russell A. Berman and Abbas Milani, with contributions from Zeyno Baran, Marius Deeb, Reuel Marc Gerecht, Ziad Haider, R. John Hughes, Nibras Kazimi, Bernard Lewis, Habib C. Malik, Camille Pecastaing, Itamar Rabinovich, Lieutenant Colonel Joel Rayburn, Lee Smith, Samuel Tadros, Joshua Teitelbaum, and Tunku Varadarajan.

BOOKS PUBLISHED UNDER THE AUSPICES OF THE
HERBERT AND JANE DWIGHT WORKING GROUP
ON ISLAMISM AND THE INTERNATIONAL ORDER

Freedom or Terror: Europe Faces Jihad
Russell A. Berman

The Myth of the Great Satan:
A New Look at America's Relations with Iran
Abbas Milani

Torn Country: Turkey between Secularism and Islamism
Zeyno Baran

Islamic Extremism and the War of Ideas: Lessons from Indonesia
R. John Hughes

The End of Modern History in the Middle East
Bernard Lewis

The Wave: Man, God, and the Ballot Box in the Middle East
Reuel Marc Gerecht

Trial of a Thousand Years: World Order and Islamism
Charles Hill

Jihad in the Arabian Sea
Camille Pecastaing

The Syrian Rebellion
Fouad Ajami

Motherland Lost: The Egyptian and Coptic Quest for Modernity
Samuel Tadros

Iraq after America: Strongmen, Sectarians, Resistance
Joel Rayburn

[For a list of essays published under the auspices of the
WORKING GROUP ON ISLAMISM AND THE INTERNATIONAL ORDER,
please see page ii.]

INDEX